When Prose Flowed Like a River

David Gregoire

BookLeaf Publishing

India | USA | UK

Presentation by *BookLeaf Publishing*

Web: www.bookleafpub.com

E-mail: info@bookleafpub.com

ISBN: 9789358315899

First edition 2023

For Christopher and Stephanie: always pursue your dreams.

ACKNOWLEDGEMENT

I'd like to acknowledge my Partner, Laurie Johnson, who challenges me, encourages me, loves me and most of all, makes me laugh.

Vacuum Tube Technology

When I was a child
Music would arrive at our radio
Like a train…
You turned the console on,
And waited…
Some faint sound, as from a distance,
Would approach upon the breeze.
You could almost see it as it blew past the
curtains,
Feel it, as it raced past us
To the cabinet of buzzing, hissing energy,
Arriving, breathless, an instant later,
A marathon runner with the news, or
Perhaps your parents favorite band,
Playing their latest hit.
Our TV worked the same.
Entertainment
Took
Time,
Back then.
It wasn't until I was older
That we broke the sound barrier,
And everything became instantly gratifying.

Jacob and the Angel

Like Jacob,
I wrestle with an Angel
Called "Self"
The inner Me whose wings,
Weighed down with chain mail trauma,
No longer fly,
But only shield that Me from
Unhappy realities,
That I created,
Trying to be safe.

So, now, when I try to access that One,
Who presides inside,
The One,
Whose wounds I hide,
The armor kinks and catches,
It deflects and snatches,
My hands.
Those leaden wings, those armored things
They obscure and hide
The child inside,
Under layer upon layer.

All day, all night I strive
To pin opinions against the earth

To finally expose the dearth
Of truth
In the stories that I was told
As whole cloth to protect
The Me
Who never grew up with dignity.

With the break of dawn,
As I lay spent, my wings are free
The chains are rent.
This angel must relearn to fly
The time is nigh!
The time is nigh!

Armoire

Words uttered in the shuttered back of a closet,
Spoken like sins in a confessional.
How much guilt do I bring to the daylight
Or hide,
Behind the wrinkled shirts of the worn stories I
tell myself?
A sturdy armoire of false narratives built to
withstand idle scrutiny,
Filled to bulging with the cardboard wings of the
angel I pretended to be,
The tarnished silver plate halo I won at church
picnic,
Where I fed dozens with two bold-faced lies
And a bottle of carbonated dreams
That tickled the nose when you drank too fast.
Delusions rolled together like mismatched
socks,
Their good intentions left hanging loose,
While the hard-core pornography of my worst
transgressions
Lay face down beneath them.
Piles of unfinished dreams,
The detritus of a life lived in fear.

Tornado

From heavy woolen clouds
Dropped a curlicue,
As from my lover's brow.
Lazy at first,
Hesitant,
Hovering between heaven and earth,
Lingering.
As tears fell from the face of the sky,
First in sorrow
Then in anguish,
The falling curl became
A figure descending,
Performing a seductive
"Danse du ventre".
Writhing as she reached for the ground,
She left me struck.

But in a FLASH,
Anguish became anger,
From Parvati came Shiva,
From cleansing came a scourge.
Twisting, turning,
A dervish of destruction,
One hand to heaven
The other to Earth,

Shredding the blameless trees
With ice and debris
With the pummeling of hail,
I froze,
Facing the fury of crazed winds,
I cowered.
Calling on God,
ANYONE,
To save me.

In answer,
Came the yawl of tortured winds so awful
That gravity itself withdrew,
And I
Lifted from the sanctuary of the ground,
Did fly!

Binocular Vision

It's been maybe a year since I looked through
binoculars,
But I thought I saw a bird that I might know,
So I just HAD to spy…
But,
By the time I found the glasses,
Removed the caps,
Adjusted the focus,
They were gone.
Leaving me fascinated by the flattened,
Two dimensional Viewmaster world outside my
window.
Pressed layers of trunk and branch,
As sharply crisp as an Autumn apple
Foreground leaves waving blurrily in front,
The background as indistinct and fuzzy as a
waking dream.
Reality strained through the lenses and prisms
Until the life is gone,
Steamrolled in "Living Color".

Ancestors in the Mist

In the pre-dawn darkness, the fog,
Dancing above the melting snow,
Is filled with the ghosts of the Grandmothers and
fathers:
Ancestors from a time before reckoning.
Graceful tendrils of mist perform pirouettes
before me
And then
Race away with the energy of a child,
For ALL that is old becomes new in the early
spring snowmelt.

Our relatives shape-shift in the fog,
Rejoicing in the birth of new life
As the frigid stasis of ice and snow yields
And our Mother's blood once more flows to
nourish the fallow land.

"Beat the drum!
Sing the songs!
We remain!
See?
We too are dancing!"

As I watch, they grow in number and size
Until I am but a mote in an opaque sea of gray
and white.
Blind,
With myriad souls surrounding me,
Whispering blessings,
Encouraging me to pray:

"Bless the water,
Our mother's mystical daughter and LOOK!
Even now it gives us form,
Lends its voice in the gentle babble of melting
ice."

…and then my vision clears
As the mists recede,
Raggy remnants playing about my feet.
The Dawn light frames my solitary self
Amidst the watery landscape.

Sow Thistle Comes to Call

I caught a sow thistle peeking in my window this
morning,
Its solar yellow blossoms just ogling me
As I set the table for breakfast,
As if to say,
"You're always looking at us,
What's your life like?"
There is no disappointment apparent upon
The petals of the blossoms
As they see the jumble and clutter of my dining
room,
Piles of vitamin bottles, store receipts,
Recent purchases that haven't found their place,
Assorted bits and bobbles.
In fact, the thistle appears to hold no judgement
Of my housekeeping at all,
Offering just a neighborly greeting…
Reaching out to connect with me
Over coffee
As the rising sun infuses us both
With energy for the day.

Snow Moon

Snow moon hanging low,
Pregnant with the Dawn.
Her upturned face, drained of all color,
Pleads to the bruised sky.

I spy her as I hurdle down roads
That cut blackened muddy swathes in the fresh
snow.
She races me, though in labor,
Always ahead,
Always beyond reach,
Until I abandon the chase.

Then she goes to ground,
Resting in a nest of treetops.
Her visage, once as of alabaster,
Reddens from her labor.
Her eyes, ever fixed on me,
Watch as I turn to leave.

Now ruddy from her effort to birth the new day,
She lay spent upon the cotton-wool landscape,
Beneath a brightening sky.

I am suspended.

Then from her womanhood to her head,
A crimson path erupts.
The time of expectation has passed
For the Sun emerges from the bloody retinue
As his mother fades,
Forgotten,
In the breaking dawn.

When Prose Flowed Like a River

I reminisce about the times
When prose flowed like a river,
A static drone unending.

Conversation was a current
Relentlessly washing our affections,
Our travails,
Our hopes
Downstream,
In a sinuous motion
Along the river bank of our day.

At times whorling in the slow shallows of
niceties,
Other times a rushing directness
That threatened to flood the moment in a deluge
of emotion,
Or meaning.

Rhyme and rhythm flashing o'er the wave tips
of inflection,
Like dragonflies,
Their wings a prism,

Separating that spectrum from meaning to
context,
And for a moment
Illuminating
Some dark space of understanding in our
souls…

Flash Flood

Hours of driving rain turned the placid river
torrid and furious,
Thirsting to take back land ceded in the summer
heat.
Coursing over road and field,
Angrily daring the fool and the naive to cross.

Invading home or business with impunity
Trumpeting in its violence:
"I am here!"

Before her, we were impotent and helpless
Standing idle and shocked,
Or praying to our craven idols,
Pleading our useless leaders,
But respite came at HER bidding,
Not ours.

And even as her campaign halted,
Her anger was evident in the roiling of the
currents:
A naked warning of her return
At a time of her bidding.

Autumn Memories

This morning, my breath was a cloud before my
face.
Iced fern fronds decorated the glass of my aged
back door,
While coarse rime trimmed it's peeling paint.

But the sun has warmed the air,
And now, at noon,
The chill lies at my feet like a corpse
Upon the patchwork forest floor.

Like the leaves, my memories lay strewn about
As I walk beneath a vault of periwinkle
Pierced by the white of an Autumnal sun.

I come upon a tribe of birches
Caught in a cascade of bright sunlight:
A tableau of stark Dalmatian trunks under
Trembling headdresses of gold.

I meander past the Liliput princess pines
Poking through the litter
And then I see my quarry:
Wintergreen.

Taking a leaf, I chew it
Transformed, I am a child.
Once more I stand with my Pepère
In the quiet woods.

Again I hear my Memère calling me home
In the chill twilight,
And feel the raspy itch of the wool quilt,
So heavy I could scarcely breathe
At bedtime in the unheated attic room,

Drowsing to her singing
"You are my Sunshine"

A Day at the Beach

The cloud hung low in the sky when we arrived
at the beach,
A purpling bruise upon the bright blue of the
sky,
Resentful of its brighter, whiter siblings,
It threatened the beachgoers beneath,
With cool winds upon damp skin and wet
clothes,
Or a machine gun spray of drops
To wound their upturned faces.
When the Sun pushed past some of the
assembled Cumuli
To warm and dry us,
This dark mass expanded to block its light
Seemingly angry that its tantrum was being
mitigated
By a bit of serene, summer Sun.
And so this pitched battle raged for an hour or so
Above us,
Until that remainder on the beach simply
stopped caring,
Picked up their things,
And left.

Wild Strawberries

A sky festooned with sober swathes of gray
above
A riot of wild greens below
Peppered with purple and white blossoms
Hovering like miniature fireworks above the
untended sward.

With a paper bag in hand,
I intrude upon this fête of weeds,
Looking for the scarlet sweetness hiding within.
At first, I see nothing of my quarry...
My search only finding its serrated heart- shaped
leaves
And a few unripe specimens among the matted
straw grass.

Doubt goads me to leave,
But I continue...

Genuflecting to the Goddess
Who blesses the ground with such a bounty of
berries
My hands move in silent supplication,
Fingers imploring the leaf tops as I search for
ripened fruit.

Prayer,
And diligence,
 Pay off

And soon I see dozens of garnet pea-sized fruits
surrounding me.
As the meadow yields this delicacy to me
My fingertips are blushed in the blood of their
ripeness,
My nose teased by the fecund sweetness
Rising as an accumulated scent from the bag.

I step gingerly twixt the miasma of grasses
Knowing that some strawberries will be pressed
Into the clay by my clumsy foot,
But regret is short-lived
In the face of the tasty bounty before me.

Labyrinth

What day do you find the Way?
What night brings a clue?
As you tread a labyrinthine path,
Or scry a pot of stew
Of bats wings, newt's eyes,
Belladonna and Rue.

How much longer whilst you wander
Before you do what you are called to?
As you walk the spiral path
Or listen for what to do.
In ocean tides, pine bough sighs,
Caterwauls or mews.

What road in the darkness leads?
What dawn reveals the truth?
As you spell the majick work
Or in the cards seek sooth,

With offerings, and open hands
True wisdom will come to you.

The Book of Dreams

Whether memories play or future foresee,
Dreaming the Book of dreams is key
To allow emotions kept under wraps
Or fantasies of places found on maps

Voluminous Tome ope unto me
An innumerable page that I may see
What the pen of Morpheus has wrought
From events of the day or what I've thought

Bound by the days of the past and to come
The leaves of the book touched by souls it has
plumbed
Look blank to the eye until the orb has read
Inscriptions of what old Morpheus has said
"Give heed! Give heed! Please listen to me!
Dreaming the Book of Dreams is key!"

Cacophony

I've heard the music of the Spheres
A cacophony from on high
It was composed of all our fears
The refrain a plaintive sigh.
Measured in a limping 2/4 time,
Peg-legged in the beat
The leaves that bore the lopsided notes,
The melted from the heat.
The gears complained, as bearings failed,
The angels went on strike.
I saw the Father, Son and Holy Ghost,
Ride off upon a bike.
But Lilith, Eve, and the Virgin Mary,
Put it all to right,
Then showered quick, coiffed their hair,
And bid us all "Good Night!"

Saturday Night Table Talk

We find ourselves in a great reveal
Passing the pipe around.
Starting with what we think we feel;
Wearing smoke like a crown.

With unintended comments giving
Our mouths the Freudian slip,
A cascade of laughter in response
Sinking our verbal ship.

For truths swan dive from off our lips
To land upon the table.
Carefree delight at sharing thoughts
We feared we'd not be able.

Mom

You come to me unexpectedly,
To knock over that pitcher in my heart
Brimming with unshed tears,
As I walk listening to books on tape.

You appear wreathed in smoke,
Your halo yellowed by nicotine
But your skin, flawless Alabaster
As when I last saw you.

Then there you are, your arm through mine
At different ages:
In your forties,
In your sixties,
Sometimes black and white,
Other times in the warmth of a Kodachrome
palette,
Young and vibrant.

Always there is fear in your eyes,
As if you knew about your end:
Blind,
The brittle bones breaking,
All couched in that constant craving for the
same dense cloud
That extinguished your Light.

If only your Love was stronger than your
addiction,
There could have been more time,
More conversations,
More laughter.

Keep me Safe

You ask me how I feel,
And I don't know…
But,
I think I know how you want me to feel.
So,
I will do my best impression of that,
If,
You'll keep me safe for a while.

Distract me from my demons…
Keep my hand from using the blade
Seeking to free the pain,
Pulsing deep within my soul.
Just,
Keep me safe for a while.

Staunch my wounded heart
Bleeding with the loss of lovers,
Or,
Stop the deluge of apocalyptic visions
From flooding my head,
As I revile my selfish act of procreation.

If you
Keep me safe

From just a few of my nightmares,
I will stay…
Take the stage,
And perform the emotions that I should…

If you keep me safe.

Concussion

There,
I see you hanging by your druthers in crimson,
Like a gamecock
Freshly taken from a crisp morning field.

My mind…
Is a
Jumbleofnonsensical
Images
And thoughts.

Weathered boards thick with grey-olive paint
Topped in maroon
Lining the walls of a dining room I've never
seen.

Thoughts that roam like Setters in the
Overgrown thicket of my mind.
Starkly in focus but for a moment before
Losing themselves in the jumble landscape.
Half-heartedly, I pursue those thoughts until a
FLASH of pain
Or
The s l o w d r y i n g glue of fatigue
distracts me
From my quarry.

Clarity,
To have clarity for just a little while and no pain.
Instead I have sedated semi-consciousness
broken
 By lapses into lucidity.

It's too hard to fight,
I am lost between worlds with no guide
Surrounded by strangers
Whose faces are familiar
But whose meanings are lost.

Words without a dictionary,
Colors without a palette.

You

You
Are so much more
Than you give yourself credit for.

Creator and creation.
You exist in the ALL:
All the tears,
All the laughter,
Both the here and ever after,
Both the finite and never ending,
You
Are it all.

In the struggles and the play
The pregnant pauses in what you say
The way your light shines undimmed
In the darkest night
When sorrows are threatening.

Creator and creation
You are the vessel
AND
The precious wine within.
The borders existing
But simply consisting

Of constructs
So you can comprehend
All that you are in.

www.ingramcontent.com/pod-product-compliance
Lightning Source LLC
LaVergne TN
LVHW010837200726

843508LV00012B/2627